THE MYSTERIES OF SPACE

GRAVITY EXPLAINED

ALEXANDER TOLISH

Enslow Publishing
101 W. 23rd Street
Suite 240
New York, NY 10011
USA

enslow.com

Published in 2019 by Enslow Publishing, LLC.
101 W. 23rd Street, Suite 240, New York, NY 10011

Copyright © 2019 by Enslow Publishing, LLC.
All rights reserved.

No part of this book may be reproduced by any means without the written permission of the publisher.

Library of Congress Cataloging-in-Publication Data

Names: Tolish, Alexander, author.
Title: Gravity explained / Alexander Tolish.
Description: New York, NY : Enslow Publishing, 2019. | Series: The mysteries of space | Audience: Grades 7 to 12. | Includes bibliographical references and index.
Identifiers: LCCN 2017051717| ISBN 9780766099500 (library bound) | ISBN 9780766099517 (pbk.)
Subjects: LCSH: Newton, Isaac, 1642-1727—Juvenile literature. | Einstein, Albert, 1879-1955—Juvenile literature. | Gravity—Juvenile literature. | Relativity (Physics)—Juvenile literature.
Classification: LCC QC178 .T595 2018 | DDC 531/.14—dc23
LC record available at https://lccn.loc.gov/2017051717

Printed in the United States of America

To Our Readers: We have done our best to make sure all website addresses in this book were active and appropriate when we went to press. However, the author and the publisher have no control over and assume no liability for the material available on those websites or on any websites they may link to. Any comments or suggestions can be sent by email to customerservice@enslow.com.

Photos Credits: Cover Andrey Armyagov/Shutterstock.com; p. 5 d1sk/Shutterstock.com; pp. 6-7 (bottom) HelenField/Shutterstock.com; p. 7 NoPainNoGain/Shutterstock.com; p. 8 posteriori/Shutterstock.com; p. 11 Universal History Archive/Universal Images Group/Getty Images; p. 13 David A. Hardy/Science Source; p. 16 Print Collector/Hulton Archive/Getty Images; p. 18 Print Collector/Hulton Fine Art Collection/Getty Images; pp. 22, 23, 25 udaix/Shutterstock.com; pp. 24, 37 adapted from diagrams provided by the author; p. 28 BlueRingMedia/Shutterstock.com; p. 30 Science & Society Picture Library/Getty Images; pp. 34, 40 Encyclopaedia Britannica/Universal Images Group/Getty Images; p. 44 Dmitrydesign/Shutterstock.com; p. 47 RFvectors/Shutterstock.com; p. 50 Mark Garlick/Science Photo Library/Getty Images; p. 53 Science History Images/Alamy Stock Photo; p. 55 Gary Hincks/Science Source; p. 58 Xinhua/Alamy Stock Photo; p. 59 NASA/ESA/STSCI/W.Colley & E.Turner, Princeton/Science Photo Library/Getty Images; p. 62 Jim Sugar/Corbis Documentary/Getty Images; pp. 65, 68 Designua/Shutterstock.com; p. 67 Yannick Mellier/IAP/Science Photo Library/Getty Images; back cover and interior pages sdecoret/Shutterstock.com (earth's atmosphere from space), clearviewstock/Shutterstock.com (space and stars).

CONTENTS

Introduction
6

Chapter One
Early Ideas About Gravity
9

Chapter Two
Isaac Newton and the Law of Universal Gravitation
20

Chapter Three:
Albert Einstein and the Special Theory of Relativity
32

Chapter Four
Albert Einstein and the General Theory of Relativity
42

Chapter Five
Experimental Tests of Relativistic Gravity
52

Chapter Six
Beyond Einstein
61

Chapter Notes 70
Glossary 74
Further Reading 76
Index 78

INTRODUCTION

Gravity is both one of the most familiar and one of the strangest forces in the universe. Since taking our first steps, we sense that something could topple us over if we do not have balance. That is gravity. Gazing through telescopes, one can see moons bound in orbits around planets, and planets around stars. That, too, is gravity. But gravity also bends the path and changes the color of light. Gravity can ripple through space, carrying news of a collision between two black holes. It can trap light from ever escaping a dying star, and it holds the key to the final fate of the universe. If it is too weak, galaxies will be ripped away from each other and isolated for eternity. However, if gravity is too strong, all matter will collapse in on itself.

Gravity is much more than the force that causes a thrown ball to fall back to Earth. It is the curvature of the universe itself. Matter and energy can "bend" the fabric of space just like a bowling ball placed on a rubber sheet will cause the rubber to sag. A marble placed on the rubber sheet will fall toward the bowling ball, mimicking the gravitational pull of a small celestial body toward one of greater mass. Or if the marble is flicked past the bowling ball, it will follow the curves of the rubber and its path will bend. Similarly, a small mass will be deflected by a larger clump of matter. This picture of gravity as curvature also

INTRODUCTION

Our solar system is made up of the sun, planets, dwarf planets, and moons. All of these heavy bodies are held together by gravity.

implies more interesting effects. If the rubber sheet is held taut, then tossing a bowling ball onto the sheet will create ripples in the sheet, spreading outward like ripples in a pond. Gravity can also behave like this. It is not just bound around heavy bodies. It can spread through space as gravitational waves.

Gravity was one of the first concepts in physics to be understood at a basic level. Isaac Newton's law of universal gravitation, which explained that apples fall from trees for the same reason that the moon goes around Earth, was one of the earliest and greatest discoveries of the Scientific Revolution.

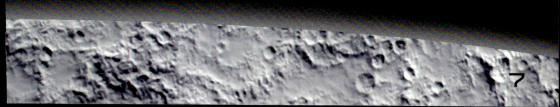

GRAVITY EXPLAINED

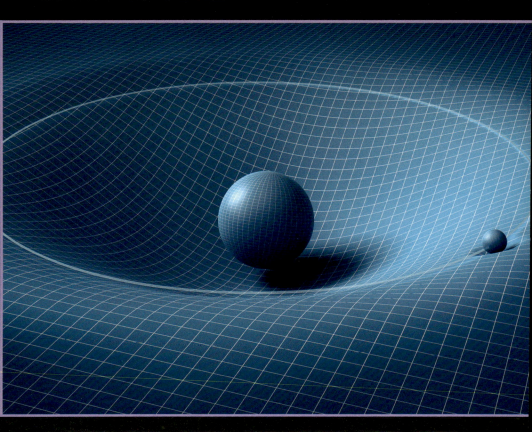

The presence of matter and energy affects the geometry of space itself, causing it to curve. This curvature affects the motion of other matter.

However, scientists are still uncertain how to combine the current theory of gravity, Albert Einstein's general relativity, with the rest of modern physics. Many of the most exciting ideas being studied today, such as extra dimensions, dark matter, and dark energy, have to do with how all of physics fits together. As scientists attempt to piece together this universal puzzle, a good place to start is with an understanding of gravity.

Chapter One

Early Ideas About Gravity

What goes up must come down. But why? This pull toward the ground is so familiar that people often take it for granted. Likewise, the sun traces a daily circle in the sky, rising in the east, crossing to the west, and passing around the other side of Earth to repeat the next day. The cycle of days and nights is a fact of life. Why does this happen? And why should anyone think that these things are related?

Curious people have sought answers to questions about the natural world for thousands of years. Ancient thinkers came up with explanations for the force pulling them to the earth and the motion of the sun, moon, and stars. These ideas evolved through the Renaissance, until one of history's greatest scientists proved that they are the same thing.

GRAVITY EXPLAINED

Aristotelian Gravity

Modern science explains nature's behavior using measurable observations. But before the scientific method was universally accepted, people tried to understand the world in other ways. Natural philosophy attempted to explain nature using logic and pure reason. One of the most important schools of natural philosophy, Aristotelian physics, grew from the work of the ancient Greek philosopher Aristotle (384–322 BCE). Aristotelians, like modern scientists, believed that the world was made up of combinations of different elements, but Aristotelian elements differed greatly from today's elements.[1]

Aristotelians believed the elements—earth, water, air, and fire—behaved as they did because of their "nature." They thought that the human world consisted of four spheres, one inside the other. The earth sphere was at the center, then water, air, and finally, fire, the outermost sphere, and elements moved, "by their nature," to rejoin their home spheres. For example, Aristotelians thought that iron was made mostly of earth, with lesser amounts of water, air, and fire. Therefore, iron should sink past fire, air, and water to reach the earth sphere at the world's center. Larger pieces of iron containing more earth would be drawn toward the earth sphere more strongly than small pieces and would fall faster. Burning wood releases fire, which rises up above the air, but also ash made of earth, which falls down. This motion of the elements to their natural homes is how the Aristotelians explained gravity.[2]

Ptolemy and Geocentricism

While this seemed to explain why everyday things rose or fell, it didn't explain the motion of the sun, moon, planets, and stars.

EARLY IDEAS ABOUT GRAVITY

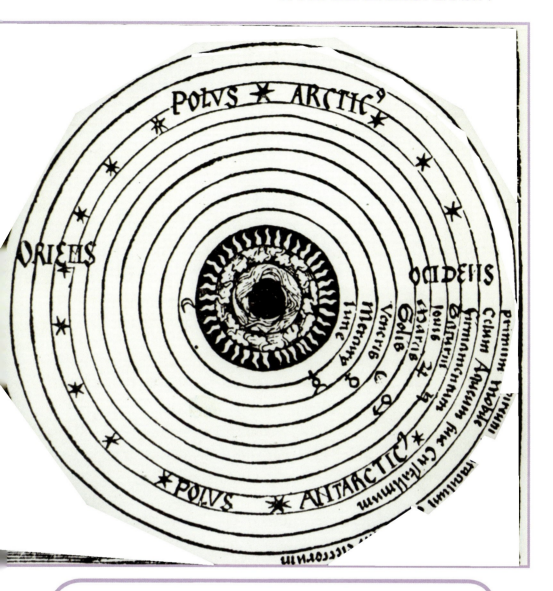

This woodcut shows the "nested spheres" of Aristotelian physics. The terrestrial spheres of earth, water, air, and fire lie at the diagram's center. They are surrounded by the spheres holding the celestial bodies.

Aristotelians believed that it was natural for matter to sit still. Things moved only to seek their home sphere (a stone thrown up always falls down). Things also moved in order to return to rest if disturbed (a stone kicked along the ground always stops).

11

GRAVITY EXPLAINED

However, the celestial bodies seemed to move in circles around the human world without stopping. Therefore, Aristotelians believed that the sun, moon, planets, and stars consisted of some fifth element, called quintessence, not present in the human world. The celestial bodies known at the time—the moon, Mercury, Venus, the sun, Mars, Jupiter, Saturn—and the distant stars were each set in concentric spheres made of this quintessence. Each sphere spun in its own way with the human world at its center. This motion had nothing to do with the gravity that pulled heavy "earthy" things to the ground, but it explained what happened in the night sky.[3]

Ancient astronomers tried to understand the motion of the spheres based on observations of the night sky. Ptolemy of Alexandria (c. 100–170), a famous and influential astronomer, collected the available observations and used Aristotelian theories as well as his own research to create the geocentric (Earth-centered) model of the universe. The regular motion of the moon, sun, and distant stars was well understood. Ptolemy even knew that the relative positions of the sun and moon created the moon's phases. However, the motion of the planets raised a problem. They also moved in repeating patterns. However, these patterns were too complicated to be explained by simple rotating spheres. There seemed to be wobbles and other variations. In fact, the word *planet* comes from the Greek word for *wanderer*, since the planets appeared to wander around where they "should" be.

Astronomers, including Ptolemy, tried to solve this problem using epicycles. They still believed that each planet's sphere rotated around Earth at a constant speed, but they added that the planets themselves traveled on much smaller circles,

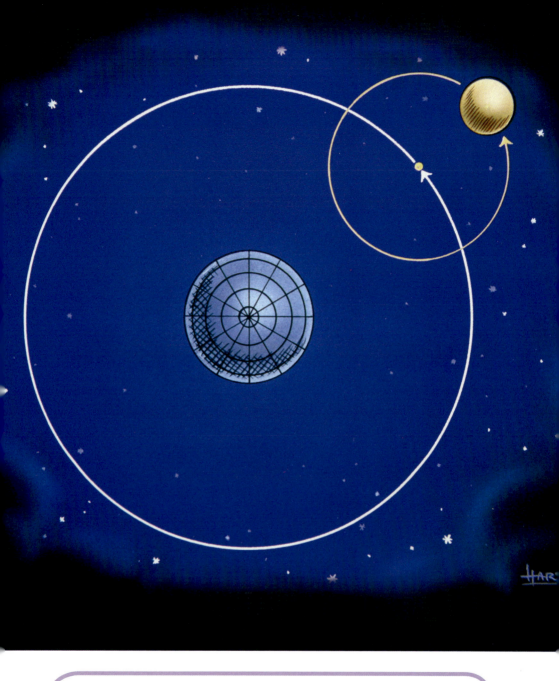

This diagram illustrates a (single) Ptolemaic epicycle. The four terrestrial spheres that make up the human realm (blue sphere) lie at the center. The crystal sphere (the large circle) holding one of the celestial bodies (yellow sphere) spins smoothly about the human realm, but the celestial body itself moves on an epicycle (the small circle) whose center (yellow dot) is fixed to the crystal sphere.

called epicycles. The epicycles' centers rotated along with the great rotating spheres. This theory agreed with the observational data. Over time, more precise observations challenged Ptolemy's geocentric model, but each time, it could be saved by adding new levels of epicycles, so that by the end of the Middle Ages, astronomers believed that the planets were moving on circles within circles within circles within circles.[4] Natural philosophers continued to struggle to recognize the universal power of gravity.

Copernicus, Kepler, Galileo, and Heliocentricism

Eventually people grew dissatisfied with the geocentric model. They realized the model had to keep changing to fit facts until it became too fuzzy. Philosophers created geocentricism to explain simply what seemed obvious: that Earth stood still while celestial bodies rotated around it. When astronomers introduced epicycles, and then epicycles within epicycles, to explain observations, the picture became too complicated.

There also seemed to be other mysterious rules that no one could explain. For example, Mercury and Venus only appeared in the sky close to the sun, so they were visible only at dawn or dusk. Mars, Jupiter, and Saturn could be seen near the sun, or late at night, when the sun was on the opposite side of Earth. Nobody knew why Mercury and Venus followed one rule but the other planets did not.

Nicholas Copernicus (1473–1543) was the first to suggest a replacement for the geocentric model. Copernicus was a true Renaissance man: lawyer, doctor, translator of ancient languages, government official, and soldier who defended Poland from

EARLY IDEAS ABOUT GRAVITY

THE SCIENTIFIC REVOLUTION

Before about 1500, most questions about the natural world were the subject of natural philosophy. Medieval and early Renaissance thinkers had so much respect for the ancient philosophers that they never questioned their basic theories. However, this began to change during the Scientific Revolution. Scholars began to use the scientific method to answer questions. The scientific method requires scientists to make a hypothesis (an educated guess at an answer), imagine and perform experiments that can disprove their hypothesis, and then change or adjust their hypothesis depending on the experiment's results. This new emphasis on experiments and observations helped prevent scientists from pursuing interesting but incorrect ideas and propelled every branch of science forward, from physics to chemistry to biology.

invasion.[5] However, he is most famous for the work he did on astronomy in his free time.

Copernicus created the heliocentric (sun-centered) model. He claimed that Earth, the other planets, and the stars went around the sun. This model still used epicycles moving on perfect spheres. However, because it made the human world

15

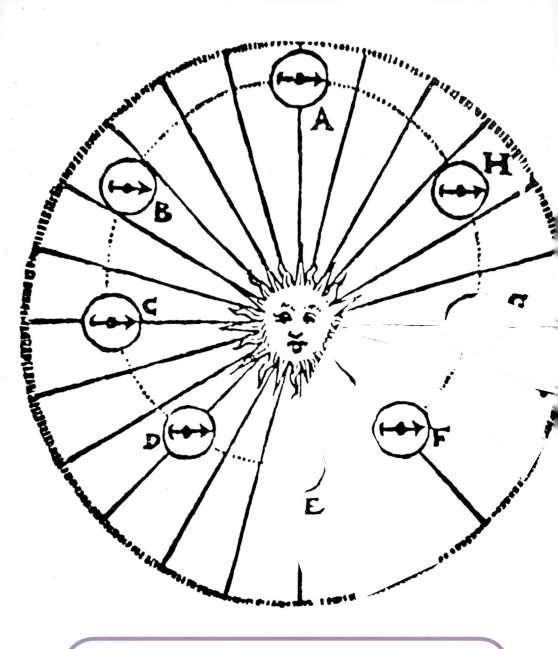

In contrast to Ptolemy and his crystal spheres centered on humanity, Kepler believed that Earth followed an elliptical (rather than perfectly circular) orbit around the sun. This image from Kepler's 1619 book *Epitome Astronomiae Copernicanae* shows celestial bodies as rotating magnets whose orbits around the sun were maintained by force field vortexes.

EARLY IDEAS ABOUT GRAVITY

one element of a larger universe instead of the universe's center, it is still regarded as one of the most important ideas in science.

Next came Johannes Kepler (1571–1630). As a boy, Kepler witnessed an eclipse predicted years earlier, which inspired him to study astronomy. A gifted mathematician, he was able to show how astronomers were able to make these predictions. His teacher, Tycho Brahe (1546–1601), had made precise observations of the planets' motion. Kepler combined this data with Copernicus's heliocentric model. He argued that the planets did not move in perfect circles with epicycles. Instead, they orbited the sun on ellipses (a special kind of oval shape) without epicycles. He also uncovered other mathematical laws, known as Kepler's laws, critical to astronomy and gravity.[6]

The first person to apply the scientific method to gravity was Galileo Galilei (1564–1642). He didn't understand that the force that attracts matter down to the ground and the force that keeps the planets moving around the sun were related. But he did conduct experiments and make observations regarding both. Another scientist would soon use his work to show that both forces were the same; both were forms of gravity.

Galileo didn't believe the Aristotelian picture of gravity as "elements seeking their home spheres." He saw that weight does not affect how quickly something falls: when it starts hailing, the first large and small hailstones hit the ground at the same time. (It is important to make the distinction between weight and mass: weight is the gravitational force acting on matter, while mass is the amount of "stuff" making up a physical object. Kilograms [kg] measure mass, and pounds [lbs] measure weight. In everyday life, metric users use "one kilogram" to mean the weight/gravitational force acting on a mass of one kilogram at Earth's surface.)

EARLY IDEAS ABOUT GRAVITY

Galileo also provided the first observational evidence that disproved the geocentric model of the planets. Telescopes had recently been reinvented in Europe. Originally, sailors used them to navigate at sea. Galileo realized he could use one to study the night sky. When looking at Jupiter, he discovered other faint specks moving back and forth around the planet. These bodies were not orbiting Earth—they were orbiting Jupiter! Jupiter must have had its own moons, which meant Earth could not be the center of the universe. Instead, Earth, Jupiter, and all the other planets moved around the sun.[7] With both mathematical theories and observational data, the scientific world was finally ready for Isaac Newton to connect all the dots and present his law of universal gravitation.

Chapter Two

Isaac Newton and the Law of Universal Gravitation

Copernicus, Kepler, and Galileo helped people think scientifically about gravity, but they weren't able to provide a bigger picture. That would have to wait for Isaac Newton (1642–1726). Newton invented calculus, which is the branch of mathematics that studies change and motion. Although other thinkers had used mathematics to describe nature, calculus allowed Newton to do more than anyone who came before. He created a scientific theory of all motion that did not distinguish between motion on Earth's surface and in the heavens. This let him show that the force that holds people on the ground and the force keeping Earth going around the sun are actually the same thing: gravity.[1]

Newton's Laws

Aristotle's theory of motion, where elements tend to return to their home sphere but matter otherwise seeks to be at rest, is based off everyday experience. A stone kicked down the road will eventually slow down and stop. Newton claimed that this doesn't have anything to do with the "nature" of the stone, but rather its surroundings. After all, a stone kicked across a frozen pond instead doesn't slow down (or at least takes longer to slow down). Matter can be slowed down by friction, but it doesn't stop by itself. Newton realized that the natural state of matter left on its own is either to remain at rest or to move with a constant velocity (uniform speed in an unchanging direction). This kind of motion is called inertial motion (inertia keeps a body at rest or moving at constant velocity). A body will remain in inertial motion unless it is acted upon by an external force. This is the first of Newton's three famous laws of motion.

The second law describes how force affects motion, quantitatively. Momentum, which equals mass time velocity, is one way to express the "strength" of motion (Which is more dangerous: getting hit by a 30-mile-per-hour (48-kilometer-per-hour) baseball or a 30-mile-per-hour car?). In Newtonian mechanics, mass doesn't change, so the first law says that the momentum of an inertial body is conserved. If an external force does act on the body, then the force equals the change in its momentum. This means that force equals mass times change in velocity, or mass times acceleration. That is, acceleration is

GRAVITY EXPLAINED

Newton's First Law
of Motion

An object at rest stays at rest and an object in motion stays in motion with the same speed and in the same direction unless acted upon by an unbalanced force.

An object at rest stays at rest

An object acted upon by a balanced force stays at rest

An object acted upon by an unbalanced force changes speed and direction

An object at rest stays at rest

An object acted upon by an unbalanced force changes speed and direction

An object in motion stays in motion

An object acted upon by an unbalanced force changes speed and direction

> Newton's first law of motion states, for example, that a large stone will stay at rest if left alone or is acted upon by a balanced force, such as a person on each side pushing against one another. The stone will only move if the two people push from the same side to create an unbalanced force. Similarly, a soccer ball will sit at rest until it is kicked, then it will fly through the air until it is stopped by the ground or a net.

in the same direction of the force and is inversely proportional to mass. So if the same force acts on an 11-pound (5-kilogram) bowling ball and a 1.8-ounce (0.05-kilogram) golf ball, both balls will accelerate in the same direction, but the acceleration of the golf ball will be one hundred times that of the bowling ball.

One important feature of the second law is that if a force acts on a body already in motion, the acceleration is combined with

ISAAC NEWTON AND THE LAW OF UNIVERSAL GRAVITATION

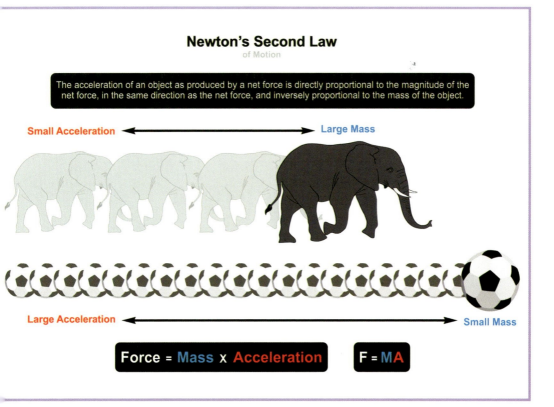

Newton's second law of motion states that the same force will cause an elephant, which has a very large mass, to accelerate much more slowly than a soccer ball, which has a relatively small mass.

the motion. For example, if a hockey puck bounces off a wall, then the wall provides a force perpendicular to itself. This force causes acceleration, and the puck's direction changes from "toward the wall" to "away from the wall." But if the puck comes in at an oblique angle, then the force doesn't affect this portion of motion; the component of velocity parallel to the wall will not change.

The force that the wall puts on the puck during the collision is perpendicular to the wall, so the perpendicular component of velocity does change. The parallel component does not.

GRAVITY EXPLAINED

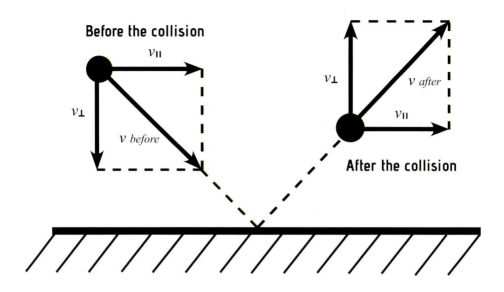

This diagram is a top-down view of a hockey puck bouncing off the wall of an ice rink. The line at the bottom of the picture with diagonal hatching beneath it simply represents the wall of the rink (a line with hatching on one side usually means "unmovable surface" in physics diagrams). The arrows represent the puck's velocity; the diagonal lines are the total velocities, and the broken lines and horizontal/vertical arrows show how the total velocities can be broken into two components: one component parallel to the rink wall ($\parallel$), and one perpendicular ($\perp$) (each with its own speed and direction). The stylized Vs (v for velocity) with the "before/after," "$\parallel$" and "$\perp$" subscripts label the different velocity vectors.

Newton's third law says that for any action, there is an equal and opposite reaction. If one body inflicts a force on another, the second body also imparts a force, of equal strength but opposite direction, on the first. For example, if someone bounces a rubber ball off the ground, clearly the ground pushes the ball up. The ball

ISAAC NEWTON AND THE LAW OF UNIVERSAL GRAVITATION

also pushes the ground—the entire planet—down. The planet's mass is so large that people can't measure its tiny acceleration. The third law also says total momentum of all matter is conserved in any physical interaction.

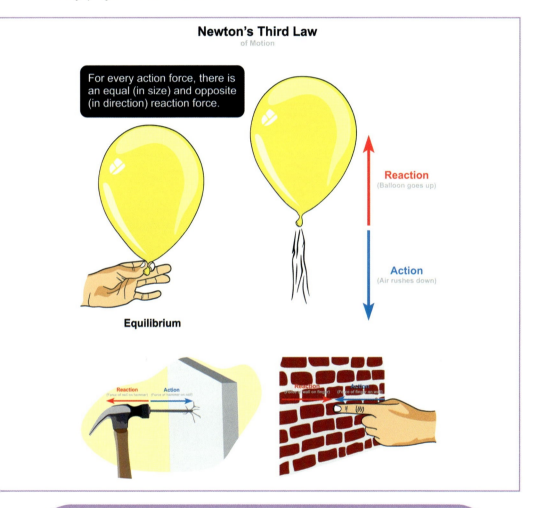

Newton's third law of motion states that as a deflating balloon pushes excess air down and out of itself, the air also pushes the balloon up, causing it to rise. Also, a hammer acts upon the nail at the same time the nail acts upon the hammer. And a person's finger pushes against the brick wall as the wall pushes against the finger.

GRAVITY EXPLAINED

Newton and the Apple

By the time that Newton investigated celestial bodies, scientists had come to accept that they were not fixed to heavenly spheres or made of special material. They were made of the same matter as everything on Earth. They should obey Newton's laws of motion as well. Kepler had shown that the planets moved around the sun on elliptical orbits, with changing speeds and directions. What kind of force could cause this acceleration?

According to legend, Newton was wandering through a garden when he saw an apple fall from a tree.[2] He asked himself why apples always fall down, rather than up or sideways. Everywhere around the planet, the force of gravity must point toward Earth's center. An apple will fall even if its tree is on a mountain top, so gravity must act over long distances. Could it reach the moon? What kind of acceleration would it cause if it did?

Consider this thought experiment. A man places a pole in the middle of a hockey rink. He ties one end of a length of rope to the pole and keeps hold of the other end. As he stands on the rink, far enough from the pole that the rope is taut, someone gives him a push. What would happen to him? In the first instant, he would start sliding, but the rope would pull him back toward the pole. He'd get a little turned, and go a little forward and a little toward the pole. In the second instant, he'd start sliding in his new direction but again get pulled back toward the pole. The process would repeat itself continuously. By constantly pulling him back toward the pole, the rope would keep him moving in a circle around the pole.

The same thing happens to the moon. Although Newton didn't understand what gravity was, he knew that it kept pulling the moon toward Earth's center of mass, just as the rope pulls

THE EQUIVALENCE PRINCIPLE

Recall Newton's second law: force equals mass times acceleration. Because the gravitational force pulling a body is proportional to the body's mass, and acceleration due to that force is inversely proportional to its mass, the body's acceleration due to gravity does not depend on its own mass. (It does depend on the mass of whatever causes the force.) This is why heavy objects don't fall faster than lighter ones: the forces acting on them are different, but they have the same acceleration. It isn't obvious why the inertial mass that relates force and acceleration in Newton's second law should equal the gravitational mass in his law of gravity, but it always does. This fact is called the equivalence principle, and it is essential to Einstein's theory of gravity.

the man toward the pole. Gravity causes the moon to fall, just as it causes the apple to fall. But the apple falls *to* Earth, while the moon keeps on falling *around* Earth.

The Inverse-Square Law

Newton understood that gravity both causes things to fall to the ground and keeps celestial bodies in cyclical motion. He also found a mathematical law that describes how strong gravity is. He proposed that the force of gravity acting between two bodies

GRAVITY EXPLAINED

is proportional to the product of their masses and inversely proportional to the square of the distance between them. This force acts on both bodies and is attractive so that they accelerate toward one another, consistent with Newton's third law of motion. Newton predicted the inverse-distance-squared

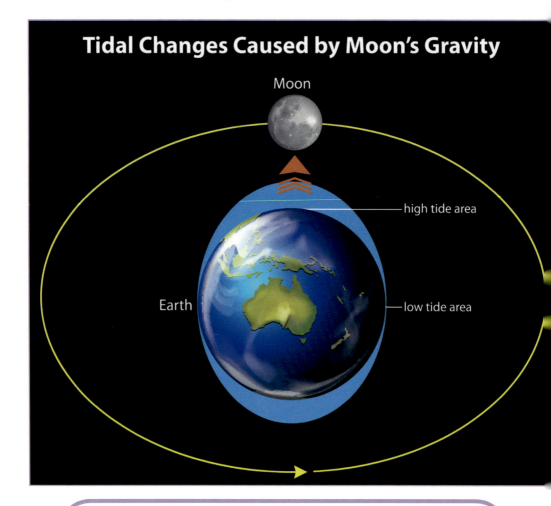

The differences in strength of the moon's gravitational pull at different points on Earth's surface causes the water in Earth's oceans and lakes to deform from a perfectly spherical shape around the planet. There is less water at low tide and more water at high tide.

dependence because this gives rise to elliptical orbits. In fact, all of Kepler's laws can be mathematically derived from Newton's law of gravity.

A person's weight is the strength of Earth's gravitational pull on her. So if a woman weighs 100 pounds (45 kg), she also attracts Earth with a 100-pound gravitational force. But when she jumps up, she falls back down; the planet doesn't "fall up" to her. The mass of Earth is almost one septillion (a one followed by twenty-four zeroes) times that of a person.[3] Therefore the acceleration of the planet toward her is about one septillion times smaller than that of her toward it. It is too small to be measured.

While the gravitational pull of Earth keeps the moon in orbit, the pull of the moon also affects life on Earth. Because gravity grows weaker at large distances, ocean water nearest to the moon feels its gravitational pull stronger than water on the opposite side of the world. Water "piles up" just beneath the moon because of this additional attraction, while on the other side, water "bulges out" because it is being pulled by the moon (toward itself, through Earth) less. These bulges keep their position relative to the moon, even as Earth rotates. People observe the water bulges twice a day as tides.

Weighing Earth

How heavy is Earth? Today, it's easy to look up the answer—about thirteen septillion pounds (six septillion kilograms).[4] But how did scientists measure the planet's mass for the first time? Newton's law provides one way. Weight is the strength of Earth's gravitational pull. It is not hard to measure something's mass, and astronomers have had reasonable estimates of Earth's radius since before Ptolemy. Is it possible to solve Newton's

GRAVITY EXPLAINED

law backward to find Earth's mass? Newton predicted that the attraction between two bodies was proportional to the product of the bodies' masses divided by the distance between them squared. He didn't know the constant of proportionality, which would allow scientists to calculate the actual strength of the force. This constant was first measured in an experiment conducted by Henry Cavendish in 1797.

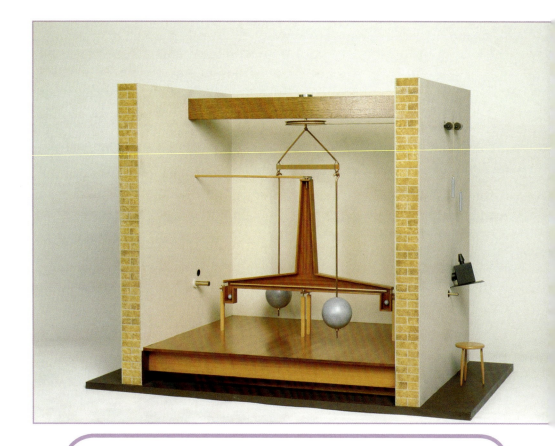

This is a model of the balance used by Cavendish to measure gravitational forces. As the suspended balls are attracted to the fixed ones, the bar from which they are suspended is forced to rotate. The angle of rotation can be measured using the pulley above the bar.

Cavendish measured the gravitational attraction between objects of known mass. He attached a light rod carrying two lead balls at each end to a heavy cable. It takes force to twist the cable, and the strength of the force can be measured by how much it twists. Cavendish placed two other fixed lead balls near the suspended balls. As the suspended balls were attracted toward the fixed ones, they forced the balance to twist until stopping. At this angle, the gravitational force attracting the balls exactly balanced the cable's resistance to twisting. Cavendish measured the angle through which it had twisted, so he knew the strength of the gravitational force. He also knew the masses of the balls and the distance between them. He was finally able to calculate the constant of proportionality in Newton's law, and through it, the mass of Earth. His results differ from today's by only about one percent.[5]

Chapter Three

Albert Einstein and the Special Theory of Relativity

Newton's laws of motion and gravitation stood as the cornerstone of mechanics for hundreds of years. They are still used by scientists and engineers today in applications from bridges to spacecraft. However, progress in other areas led scientists to question Newton's laws on a fundamental level. By the early twentieth century, it had become clear that while they remained valid on everyday scales, they needed to be modified when describing high-speed motion. Albert Einstein (1879–1955) proposed a new theory of motion—relativity—that addressed these concerns and radically changed the way scientists think about space, time…and gravity.

The Michelson-Morley Experiment

By the late nineteenth century, scientists knew that light is a kind of wave. Waves show up frequently in physics. All the waves studied before needed a medium to travel through: water waves travel through the water, and sound waves travel through gasses such as the air. Scientists assumed light must be similar. There must be some medium, which they called aether, through which light waves travel. This aether was thought to be present throughout the entire universe and to coexist with matter, as light can travel through solids (like glass), liquids, and gases, as well as the vacuum of space.

A medium's motion affects the speed of waves traveling through it: sounds can be "carried" by the wind and travel farther in the direction of the wind than they would on a breezeless day. The same should be true for light in the aether: if Earth moves through the aether as it orbits the sun, then people on Earth will experience an "aether wind" like the rush of air past a person riding in a convertible car with the top down. Light should speed up (if it is carried by the aether wind), slow down (if it travels against the wind), or remain nearly unaffected (if it travels perpendicular to the wind). Scientists in the nineteenth century designed experiments to measure such directional variations in the speed of light.

The most precise experiment was conducted by Albert Michelson (1852–1931) and Edward Morley (1838–1923) in 1887.[1] They used a device called an interferometer. An interferometer uses mirrors to split a beam of light into two, which travel down two perpendicular arms of equal length. At the end of the arms are additional mirrors, which reflect the two beams back toward

33

GRAVITY EXPLAINED

the splitter, where they are recombined into one. If the two split beams have traveled at the same speed, when they recombine they will be in-phase and the recombined beam will be as bright as the original beam. However, if the two have different speeds, when they are recombined they will be out-of-phase and the recombined beam will be dimmer. Using an interferometer,

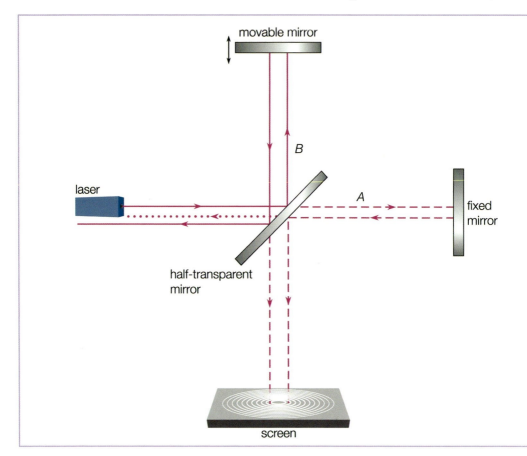

This illustration depicts the sort of interferometer used by Michelson and Morley when they tried to measure the aether wind. If the wind had "blown" in either direction A or B, the speed of light in that direction would have changed, which would have affected the display on the screen. This was not observed.

Michelson and Morley tried to measure the effect of the aether wind on the speed of light. They assumed that an arm pointing east-west (parallel to the direction of Earth's rotation and orbit around the sun) would experience an aether wind, while an arm pointing north-south (perpendicular to these directions) would not: the recombined beam should be weak. They instead observed that the speed of light was the same in both directions. Unlike more familiar waves, light's speed does not depend on its motion through any medium. Michelson and Morley had failed to measure what they were investigating. This "failure" would soon prompt Einstein to develop the theory of relativity.

Space, Time, and Space-time

Some scientists tried to explain the Michelson-Morley results by modifying the aether theory. Einstein discarded it altogether. He proposed that light simply doesn't need a medium. Since there is no question of the relative speed of the wave source with respect to the medium, all light waves travel at the same speed. This is even more revolutionary than it sounds. It means that if a spaceship fires a beam of light (with speed of one foot per nanosecond[2]), and a second spaceship traveling in the same direction at one-half the speed of light observes this beam, the second ship will also measure the light moving at one foot per nanosecond. This is completely contradictory to everyday understanding of motion, and Einstein had to introduce a very new understanding of what space and time are to have it make sense.

Einstein believed that space and time are not separate things. Instead, they are two different aspects of one thing: space-time. To get a sense of what this must mean, imagine a

GRAVITY EXPLAINED

man who cannot walk in any direction at any speed he chooses. Instead, he can only make 10-centimeter steps to the east and west, and 1-meter leaps to the north and south. He cannot make steps between the cardinal directions. A normal person, without these encumbrances, would think of the cardinal directions as convenient labels, but no more; a mile-long walk will be a mile long, no matter what direction it's in. But our particular man will not see things this way. He might think that north and south are fundamentally different from east and west. For example, imagine that he finds two pole-vaulting poles. One extends 30 steps (300 centimeters) east and 4 leaps (4 meters) north tip to tip, while the other measures 40 steps (400 centimeters) and 3 leaps (3 meters). He might be confused to hear that these two poles are identical. However, someone else who was familiar with the Pythagorean theorem would realize that the lengths of the poles could be calculated as the hypotenuses of two right triangles, one with legs of 3 and 4 meters, and other with legs of 4 and 3 meters. This person would understand that both poles are 5 meters long; they are simply rotated in slightly different directions.

Humans have a similar difficulty with space-time. The speed of light sets the "exchange rate" between space and time (because light travels at one foot per nanosecond, one foot equals one nanosecond). Because human life takes place at speeds far below that of light, it's very difficult to see precisely how space and time are related. However, at high speeds, motion through space affects motion through time. Someone moving at nearly the speed of light will be seen by an observer at rest to be traveling through time more slowly than himself. For example, if he were to examine the watch of a woman running nearly the speed of light, he would see it marking much less than one minute within what he regarded as a minute. This is called time dilation.

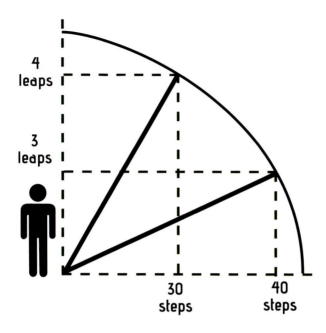

Two poles are the same length; they can both be radii of a single circle. They're just pointing in different directions. We can see that "leaps" and "steps" are different units/labels/coordinates for the same thing (length). But if someone is unable to recognize this, then what we see as a simple rotation (which doesn't change anything about the pole itself) will look like a mysterious "width dilation" and "height contraction." Just like in special relativity, if someone doesn't recognize that both "meters" and "seconds" are two different units/labels/coordinates for the same thing (space-time interval), then motion (which doesn't change anything about a body itself) will look like a mysterious "time dilation" and "length contraction."

Time dilation is one of the clues that led Einstein toward special relativity.[3] He speculated what the world would look like if he chased after and caught up with a beam of light. Since light is a wave, if he were running alongside it with the same speed, it

GRAVITY EXPLAINED

shouldn't be moving, but standing still. This is impossible according to the laws that describe light. Therefore time itself must "stand still" to an observer traveling at the speed of light. After combining this insight with the results of the Michelson-Morley experiment, he was able to announce the full special theory of relativity.

Another consequence of special relativity related to time dilation is called length contraction. A body traveling near the speed of light will appear to be "squished" in the direction of motion. Think back to how a 5-meter pole can be expressed in either 30 steps and 4 leaps or 40 steps and 3 leaps. If someone were to rotate the pole, he would change "leaps" into "steps" or vice versa without actually changing the pole. Movement is a sort of rotation within space-time. It can mix together "distance" and "duration." According to an observer at rest, the amount of time it takes for the runner's watch to show that a minute has passed will take longer, but the diameter of her watch parallel to the direction will shrink.

Experimental Tests of Special Relativity

Special relativity needed to be experimentally tested before it became good science. Even though humanity has never reached speeds near that of light, very precise equipment can measure small time dilations at lower speeds. In 1971 Joseph Hafele (1933–2014) and Richard Keating (1941–2006) brought atomic clocks aboard a jet and flew around the world at high speeds. When they landed, they found their clocks showed slightly earlier times than the standard atomic clock held at the US Naval Observatory. Their high-velocity clocks had moved through time more slowly than the low-velocity earthbound clock, as Einstein had predicted.[4]

SPECIAL RELATIVITY AND RADIOACTIVITY

Even though scientists can't approach the speed of light, they can study other things that do, such as cosmic rays. Cosmic rays are particles such as muons created in subatomic reactions in outer space, and they constantly rain on Earth at high speeds. Muons are radioactive: after being created, they decay into other particles and emit energy. Scientists know how long, on average, muons created in laboratories on Earth exist before decaying, and cosmic muons live much longer than this. This is because decay takes place according to the muons' internal time, not the scientists' laboratory time. Since cosmic muons travel at great speeds, their lifetimes seem stretched to observers nearly at rest.[5]

Scientists have also observed length contraction. Particle physicists collide atoms and subatomic particles at very high speeds and detect what comes out of the collision. The paths of the outgoing particles depend on their sizes and shapes. Some particles, naturally spherical at low velocities, scatter like flat disks. Scientists explain this by saying that the particles' diameter in the direction of motion is contracted. They call this process "pancaking" since the particles are squished into the shape of pancakes.[6]

GRAVITY EXPLAINED

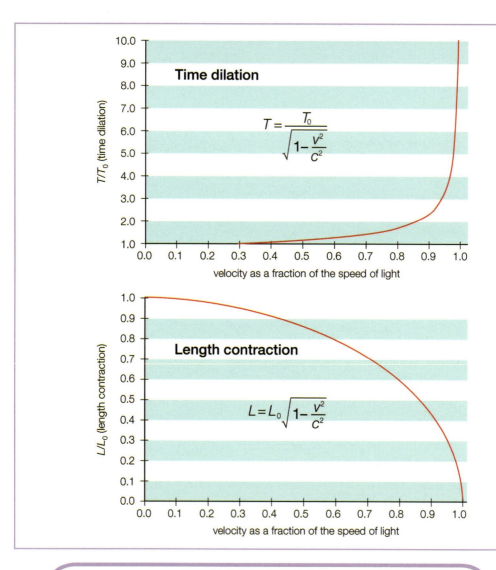

These graphs depict how space and time can be "stretched" in the theory of relativity. An observer sitting at rest sees a runner approaching the speed of light (moving along the x-axes of the graphs to 1.0). The amount of time it takes for the observer to see one second marked on the runner's watch (the y-value of the first graph) increases to infinity. The length of a meter stick, carried by the runner parallel to the direction of his running (the y-value of the second graph), appears to the observer to shrink to zero length.

Laws of Motion in Special Relativity

Despite how much special relativity has changed the way scientists view space and time, Einstein's laws of motion are similar to those of Newton. Newton's first law, which states that bodies remain in inertial motion unless acted upon by an external force, remains in effect. The theory of relativity adds that all inertial observers agree on all physical laws, including the speed of light. Force still equals change in momentum, as in the second law, although momentum in the theory of relativity does not simply equal mass times velocity. It also includes another factor, nearly constant at one for low velocities but approaching infinity near the speed of light. Therefore at low speeds, force very nearly equals mass times change in velocity (as Newton said), but near the speed of light, force almost entirely goes into changing this factor instead of velocity. It is physically impossible to accelerate something past the speed of light. The third law is also valid: total relativistic momentum is conserved.

Although special relativity contains strange new effects such as time dilation, scientists are able to use old ideas such as momentum and force to describe how matter behaves. Space-time is more complicated than the pre-relativistic picture of space and time, but it is still just a background environment. Space-time itself was not interesting; interesting things happened within space-time. This changed when Einstein tried to incorporate gravity into relativity: he found that space-time can take on a life of its own.

Chapter Four

Albert Einstein and the General Theory of Relativity

instein's special theory of relativity may have replaced Newton's laws of motion, but what about Newton's law of gravity? It says that there is an attractive force between any two bodies that depends on their masses and the distance between them. It does not try to explain what causes this force or how it can extend over astronomical distances. It only states that the force instantaneously "happens." This had always troubled physicists. It was also irreconcilable with special relativity, which states that nothing happens faster than light. Einstein called Newton's law of gravity "spooky action at a distance"[1] and tried to explain gravity in a way that was compatible with relativity.

His starting point was the equivalence principle: a body's acceleration due to gravity does not depend on that body's mass. All matter behaves identically within the same gravitational field. Because of this, Einstein believed that gravity isn't simply an interaction between two bodies. It is actually an interaction between each body and space-time itself. Matter "does something" to space-time, and space-time "tells" matter how to move. He explained this idea in his general theory of relativity: gravity is the geometrical curvature of space-time.

Curvature

What is curvature? While the "curvature of space-time" is abstract, it can be understood by beginning with something familiar—two-dimensional surfaces within a three-dimensional world. Think about the surface of Earth (which is two-dimensional, even if Earth itself is a three-dimensional ball). On small scales— say, the size of a city—and ignoring things like hills and valleys, the ground seems to be flat and to obey Euclidean geometry. The shortest path between two points (mathematicians call this a geodesic) is a straight line, and two straight roads that run parallel to one another will remain the same distance apart from each other.

On large scales, where Earth is clearly spherical, things are different. The geodesics of a sphere are great circles—circles on the surface of the sphere that have the same center as the sphere. The lines of longitude on a globe (running north–south) are geodesics, but the lines of latitude (except for the equator) are not. Therefore a flight between Chicago and Rome, which both lie on the same line of latitude (41.5 degrees north), will not stay on this line, but instead follow the great circle linking the

GRAVITY EXPLAINED

The straightest line segment or shortest distance between two points can appear bent or bowed when the two points lie in a curved region such as Earth's surface.

two cities. The shortest flight path between the two cities will look like an arc rather than a straight line on a cylindrically projected map (which shows lines of latitude and longitude as a regular grid). If the flight appears to take a longer trip than necessary,

ALBERT EINSTEIN AND THE GENERAL THEORY OF RELATIVITY

that is the fault of the map, not the pilot. On curved surfaces, straight lines (geodesics) do not obey Euclidean expectations.

Topographical maps—two-dimensional maps that depict elevation using rings to denote constant height—provide another way to think about curvature. Imagine a tired hiker who's seen enough nature and just wants to get back to camp on the other side of a hill. Someone else, watching her progress on a topographical map without understanding what the rings mean, would advise her to make a beeline for camp: after all, the shortest distance between any two points is a straight line. The hiker disagrees. She knows that hiking uphill is more difficult than walking over level ground, so that, as far as she is concerned, one mile on the hill is as bad as two miles off of it. She will walk around the hill, but she won't think of it as going out of her way. Her path of least resistance is bent, according to an outside observer, by the curvature of the land.

Space-time Curvature

Space-time, like a surface, can be flat or curved. Think back to the space-time of special relativity: here, inertial particles move in straight lines through space and time at constant speeds. They move upon geodesics of the space-time and only wander off the geodesics if acted upon by a force. These geodesics obey common sense intuition about straight lines (initially parallel trajectories remain parallel, etc.) similar to the Euclidean intuition of the flat plane. Therefore physicists say that the space-time of special relativity is flat.

But what does it mean for space-time to be curved? A curved space-time is one whose geodesics do not obey inertial intuition. As in flat space-times, bodies not experiencing external forces

GRAVITY EXPLAINED

are said to be in inertial motion, and inertial bodies still follow geodesics. But, as was the case for the transatlantic flight and the tired hiker, these geodesics may not look straight. This apparent non-straightness is interpreted as acceleration due to gravity.

If it is not clear what this curvature has to do with the attractive gravitational force of Newton, consider the rubber sheet analogy from this book's introduction. Imagine a large rubber sheet held taut. On the middle of the sheet sits a bowling ball, causing the sheet to sag in the center. If someone were to flick a marble along the edge of the sheet, far from the sagging, its path will be nearly straight. However, if he flicked it nearer to the bowling ball, he would see its trajectory arc as it enters the sag and then straighten—in a different direction—after emerging from the other side of the sag. The closer he flicked the marble to the bowling ball, the greater the arc and the more dramatic the change in direction. It is possible to flick the marble so that it loops back toward the flicker. It is even possible, if friction is negligible and he began the marble in the proper position with the proper initial velocity, to get it to circle around the bowling ball repeatedly, like a planet orbiting a star. Of course, this analogy is not perfect. The rubber sheet is a two-dimensional surface curved within a larger three-dimensional space; in fact it requires gravity as an external force to work. However, gravity is just keeping the marble on the sheet. It's the sheet's geometry that is actually influencing the marble's motion.

Now imagine that this sheet is marked with a regular grid while it is flat, so that the grid lines are separated by one inch. When the bowling ball is present, the grid will be stretched along with the sheet. Although the grid can still be used to label points on the sheet, it will not be an accurate measure of distance. An inch according to the grid lines near the bowling ball, measured

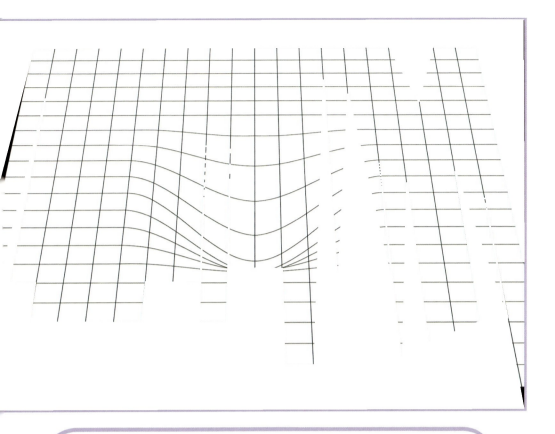

This surface is labeled with coordinate-like grid lines, which mark inches of real distance when they are far away from the deforming curvature. Where the curvature is strong, these "inch labels" are stretched and do not mark real, physical inches.

with a ruler, will actually be longer than an inch. It is likewise within general relativity. The curvature of space-time does not only cause geodesics to bend, it can also cause space and time to "stretch" relative to what an observer in flat space-time would expect. The result is that gravity can cause time dilation and length contraction, similar to high-speed motion in special relativity. A clock on Earth's surface measures time more slowly than a clock in orbit.

GRAVITY EXPLAINED

Einstein realized that, because matter tries to follow space-time's geodesics, the space-time's geometrical curvature tells matter how to move. But this was just one half of the story. Matter (and other forms of energy) tells space-time how to curve. He wanted a mathematical law that described the relationship between the density of "stuff" and the presence of curvature, just like Newton's law of gravity described the relationship between

GLOBAL POSITIONING SYSTEM (GPS)

Progress in physics often leads to practical inventions. How can something like space-time curvature be used in everyday life? The Global Positional System (GPS) is a network of artificial satellites orbiting Earth. Each carries an atomic clock and broadcasts nanosecond ticks on radio waves. A GPS receiver (or a car or phone with a built-in receiver) measures these signals from multiple satellites and uses their relative positions to find (or triangulate) its own position on Earth's surface. The most advanced GPS receiver systems are accurate to within inches. This requires incredibly precise communication between satellites and receivers. However, gravity will change the timing of the atomic clock as seen from Earth. The timing would appear so off that the most precise GPS receiver would be inaccurate within two minutes without a general relativistic understanding of gravity.[2]

mass and force. For weak, slowly changing gravitational fields, Einstein's own geometrical law of gravity must approximate Newton's law, just like special relativity approximates Newton's laws of motion at low speeds. Eventually, Einstein came up with a satisfactory law, which is now known as the Einstein equation. He finally knew how matter causes space-time to curve. This, along with the geometrical ideas of geodesics, forms the general theory of relativity. Special relativity, which deals only with flat space-times, is a special case of general relativity.

Other Forms of Gravity

Gravity surrounding an isolated massive body is one solution to the Einstein equation, known as the Schwarzschild solution. However, other solutions are also valid gravitational fields. The rubber-sheet analogy illustrates how the geometrical idea of gravity explains the attractive force studied for hundreds of years, but it can also help demonstrate other forms of gravity unknown to Newton.

For example, gravitational waves are another solution to the Einstein equation. When very heavy bodies interact—such as two black holes colliding—they create ripples of curvature spreading throughout the universe. This too can be seen using the rubber sheet. If you release two bowling balls from opposite sides of a taut sheet, they will "attract" each other to the sheet's center and then collide. The violence of their collision will create little shock waves in the rubber, traveling away from the collision. The curvature of these shock waves can be measured, and it will cause distant light bodies, such as marbles, to move, but it is not straightforwardly "attractive" like the bowling ball sag is.

GRAVITY EXPLAINED

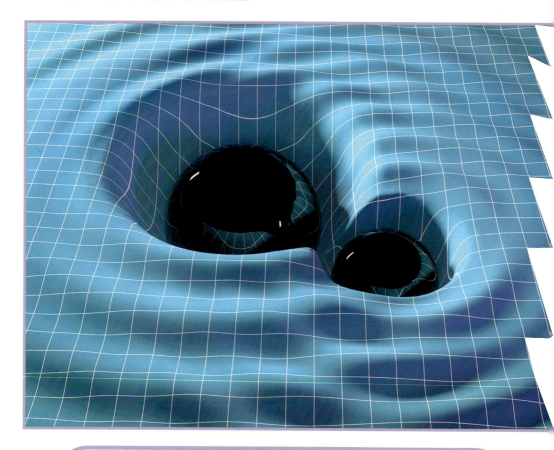

When heavy bodies interact, such as two black holes colliding, their "curvature sags" can ripple away from the bodies themselves, like waves spreading away from a stone tossed into a pond. These ripples of space-time curvature are gravitational waves.

Gravitational waves are similar. They radiate through space-time without being bound as an attractive force to any single star or planet.

Curvature also explains the large-scale structure of the universe. The usual objects of astronomy—stars, planets, moons, and so on—tend to attract themselves. If there were nothing else going on, all the visible matter would fall together and merge. But astronomers do not see this happening. Instead, distant galaxies move apart at ever faster speeds. Imagine if our rubber sheet were actually the surface of a rubber balloon marked with a grid, and that the balloon is being inflated. Points on the grid are pushed apart. Similarly, the cosmos is being made to expand, and galactic clusters are pushed away from each other. Scientists do not understand what causes this expansion. Until they do, they will never be certain whether the universe will continue expanding forever—or whether the attractive forces will catch up and cause the universe to collapse in on itself.

Chapter Five

Experimental Tests of Relativistic Gravity

A scientific theory is only as good as the testable predictions it makes. General relativity is no different. A statement like "space-time is curved" is difficult to verify directly, as there is no way that scientists can leave space-time in order to compare it to a separate flat space-time. Instead, theorists study relativity to predict effects occurring within space-time that can be explained by Einstein's gravity-as-curvature picture, but not by other models of gravity.

Perihelion Shift

The first phenomenon used to justify relativity was observed by astronomers before Einstein was even born. Within Newtonian

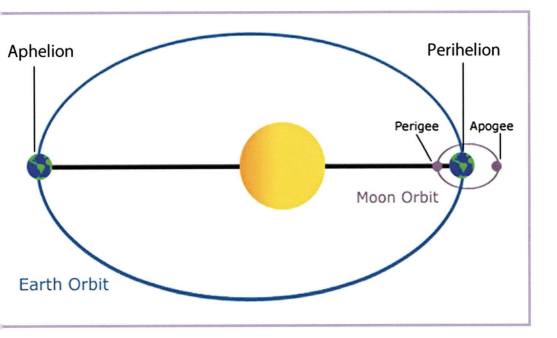

A planet's closest approach to its parent star is called its perihelion. This diagram shows Earth's perihelion as well its aphelion, its farthest point from the sun. The motion of Mercury's perihelion demonstrated that Einstein's theory of gravity is more accurate than Newton's theory.

gravity, the orbit of a planet around its star is said to be closed, meaning that one loop ends precisely where it begins. If the orbit is elliptical, then its closest point to the star—called its perihelion— must not change over time. If there are multiple planets in the solar system, each being pulled upon by each other as well as by the star, then the planets' perihelia will slowly but steadily shift around the star orbit after orbit. Astronomers were able to measure this perihelion shift, but by the middle of the nineteenth century, they knew the rate at which Mercury's perihelion shifted was not consistent with Newtonian predictions.

GRAVITY EXPLAINED

At first, physicists tried to explain this anomaly by adding new forces from hypothetical undiscovered planets without changing the underlying Newtonian physics.[1] Einstein used these observations to guide himself as he searched for the Einstein equation. He kept on modifying the mathematics of his law until it accurately predicted the observed shift in Mercury's perihelion. Since then, astronomers have found that relativity also predicts the perihelion shift of other planets more accurately than Newtonian gravity.

Redshifting

The "stretching" of space by gravity can have significant observable effects on electromagnetic waves such as light. Waves are characterized by, among other things, their wavelength, or the distance between neighboring peaks. (For waves such as those in water, the meaning of "peak" is obvious. For more abstract waves, such as the air-pressure waves that make up sound or electromagnetic waves, a peak is a position of maximum intensity: where the pressure is highest in a sound wave or where the electromagnetic field is strongest in light.) The color of light is determined by its wavelength: if the light has a wavelength of 450 nanometers, it is blue; if it has a wavelength of 700 nanometers, it is red. (Light of wavelengths less than 380 or greater than 750 nanometers are not visible with the human eye, although physicists still call them "light.") Gravity can stretch the wavelength of a light beam and change its color. It is more common to see light shifted to a longer wavelength, in the direction of red, so the process is usually referred to as "redshifting."

EXPERIMENTAL TESTS OF RELATIVISTIC GRAVITY

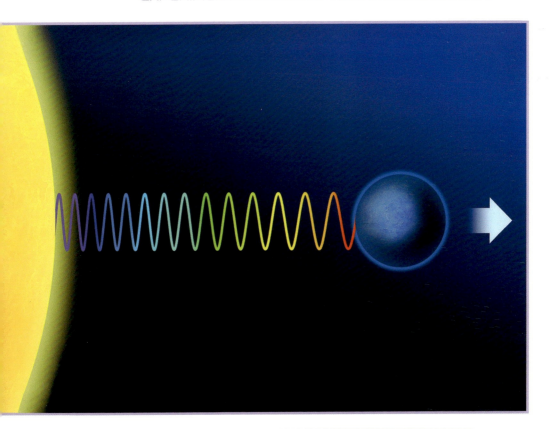

Light gets stretched to a longer wavelength and loses energy as it climbs out of a gravitational well, as illustrated by the observer (blue sphere) moving away from the yellow star. Color is shifted along the spectrum. Blue lights get moved toward red, and red lights become infrared, which are not visible to the naked human eye.

Scientists have observed redshifting on Earth's surface, although neither the light they used nor the change in its wavelength was visible to the human eye. Using a nuclear process that emits a specific wavelength of light and a precise detector, they found that light is very slightly redshifted as it shines from the bottom of a tower to its top.[2] Cosmological redshifting, which occurs

GRAVITY EXPLAINED

as the universe expands, is more dramatic. The wavelength of light in an expanding space-time is like the spacing between grid lines on a rubber balloon: as the universe expands, the light's wavelength will be stretched along with it. Therefore light coming from distant galaxies, which has been traveling through much cosmic expansion, should be significantly redshifted with respect to light coming from nearby stars, which has traveled through less expansion. Astronomers confirm this.[3]

Gravitational Waves

One of Einstein's most radical predictions was the existence of gravitational waves—space-time curvature traveling freely, unbound to any massive body. Scientists agreed the most effective method to detect waves would be an interferometer, the same device used in the Michelson–Morley experiment that prompted relativity.

This proposed experiment also split a light beam down two perpendicular, equal-length arms and analyzed the recombined signal. Scientists knew from Michelson and Morley that, under normal circumstances, the split beams would take equal travel times and reunite in-phase, creating a strong signal. They now predicted that, if a gravitational wave were to pass the interferometer as the experiment ran, the traveling curvature would stretch one arm longer than the other. The beams would take different travel times and would not recombine in-phase. The final signal would weaken until the wave passed. Ironically, while the original Michelson–Morley result proved the necessity of relativity, its failure here would corroborate one of relativity's strangest predictions.

This was more easily said than done. Physicists estimate that gravitational waves passing through Earth squeeze space by a factor of about a sextillionth (one divided by a one with twenty-one zeroes).[4] Trying to measure this is like trying to measure the variation of a proton's diameter in the distance from sea level to the deepest trench in the ocean—while the sea's surface is sloshing above.

THE LASER INTERFEROMETER GRAVITATIONAL-WAVE OBSERVATORY (LIGO)

As difficult as it is to detect a gravitational wave, it has been done. In the autumn of 2015, a century after Einstein first proposed the general theory of relativity and raised the possibility of gravitational waves, the scientists of the Laser Interferometer Gravitational-Wave Observatory (LIGO) detected the waves created by the collision of two black holes, each about thirty times the mass of the sun, more than a billion light-years away from Earth—well outside the Milky Way galaxy.[5]

The LIGO experiment uses two state-of-the-art interferometers, in Louisiana and Washington State. Only if both interferometers

(continued on the next page)

GRAVITY EXPLAINED

(continued from the previous page)

detect a signal do the scientists investigate it as a possible gravitational wave. Using data from both sites also helps the team detect what direction in the sky the wave came from. LIGO continues to detect additional gravitational waves and collect vital data.

This is one of the LIGO detectors, in Livingston, Louisiana. It is a two-armed interferometer, just like the kind used by Michelson and Morley. However, the LIGO interferometers must be much larger in order to detect extremely weak gravitational waves from space.

EXPERIMENTAL TESTS OF RELATIVISTIC GRAVITY

Gravitational Lensing

Light has no mass. Therefore it cannot be affected by Newtonian forces. This is not the case within relativity: light beams travel upon geodesics, just like massive matter. Since gravity bends all geodesics, it bends the path of light. This can be tested using starlight. Astronomers know where the stars "should be" in the sky, so if a heavy body passes near Earth's line of sight to a star and the star appears to move, then the gravitational field of the body must have bent the starlight. This is known as gravitational lensing.

The cluster of yellow-orange colored galaxies in the middle of the image creates a strong lensing field. Light coming from a farther galaxy is bent and distorted by the field, resulting in the blue images surrounding the cluster.

GRAVITY EXPLAINED

During the day, the sun is so bright that other stars are invisible. On the other hand, the moon is so light that its effect on the trajectory of light is not measurable. When Einstein proposed general relativity in 1915, the only possible way to observe the bending of light was to wait for a total eclipse of the sun. Because of the sun's great mass, starlight traveling close by it would be visibly bent, but the moon would block the sun's own light, making the bent starlight visible on Earth. The astronomer Arthur Eddington (1882–1944) was the first to test this prediction in Brazil. He found that, during the eclipse, the stars did indeed appear to wander off. Regarding the incident, the *New York Times* warned its readers: "Stars Not Where They Seemed or Were Calculated to Be, but Nobody Need Worry."[6]

Chapter Six

Beyond Einstein

So far, Einstein's theory of relativity has passed every test scientists have imagined. But physicists know that general relativity is not the final word on gravity. They work to find a broader theory that contains general relativity as a special case, just as relativity contains Newton's laws of motion and gravity as slow-motion and weak-gravity special cases. Expanded theories of gravity have many features that aren't a part of Einstein's picture.

Artificial Gravity

Most science-fiction movies with astronauts on spaceships show them walking on the floor no differently than people on Earth. This is not what actually happens. Astronauts float around their vessel; gravity doesn't hold them down. Gravity does act on both astronauts and their ships, keeping them bound in orbit. But because it acts on them equally, in accordance with the equivalence principle, they fall around Earth together. The same

Contemporary space agencies already use simple tricks to simulate gravity and weightlessness well within Earth's atmosphere, primarily to train astronauts, but occasionally to assist science-fiction movie makers. Pictured here is a training vessel that flies to a high altitude then steeply dives toward Earth. Passengers fall to Earth along with the plane and thus feel weightless with respect to their environments (like a doomed rider in a falling elevator).

thing happens in an elevator if its cable snaps: gravity does not hold any unfortunate passenger to the elevator's floor, since it is pulling the elevator itself down the shaft equally quickly. The rider will feel weightless with respect to his immediate surroundings (the elevator car).

Scientists and engineers have thought about how to simulate a gravity-like force toward the floor on spacecraft for the benefit of astronauts. One idea, for ships traveling between planets, is to keep the ship accelerating for the whole trip.[1] Astronauts and cargo, not having thrusters of their own, will naturally tend to travel at constant velocities. An inertial observer outside the ship will see the rear of the ship, being accelerated forward, push up against the matter within the cabin. On the other hand, an observer within, using the ship's interior as a frame of reference, will see things fall to the ship's rear as if there were a gravitational pull. However, it would take too much fuel to fire the ship's thrusters for such a long period of time.

A rotating vessel could also simulate gravity.[2] This would work in a way similar to a playground merry-go-round. A child holding onto a spinning merry-go-round will feel an outward pull. There is no real outward force; the child will tend to move inertially, with constant velocity, but within the spinning merry-go-round's frame of reference this will seem to be moving away from the axis of rotation. This effect is called a centrifugal (center-fleeing) force, although again, there is no actual force. In the case of a rotating spaceship or space station, centrifugal force will cause astronauts and cargo to fall away from the axis, so that the "ground" will actually be the cylindrical outer wall.

Quantum Gravity

General relativity is very good at describing big things such as stars and galaxies. Scientists do not know how well it describes tiny things such as protons and electrons. They don't know how to design experiments that test gravity at such small scales. On a theoretical level, however, general relativity is incompatible with quantum theory, which is the branch of physics that describes very small things. Quantum theory ascribes a certain kind of randomness to the universe. Even empty space is full of potential particles hopping in and out of existence. These potential particles still have energy, so they cause space-time to curve, just like more familiar forms of matter. However, this picture of space-time, violently boiling at infinitely small scales, contradicts the smooth, calm geometry that physicists observe in the macroscopic world. One of the most active areas of theoretical physics is exploring how to reconcile the relativistic understanding of gravity-as-curvature with the quantum principle of small-scale randomness.

One of the earliest attempts to think about gravity on very small scales was the Kaluza–Klein theory. Theodor Kaluza (1885–1954) and Oskar Klein (1894–1977) believed that there is a fifth dimension (in addition to the three known spatial and one time dimensions) that is rolled into a tiny circle. This extra dimension is so small that humans cannot observe it in everyday life, just like a telephone wire looks like a one-dimensional line from far away, even though it is made of three-dimensional material. Space-time is curved in all five dimensions, but only curvature in the four macroscopic dimensions looks like familiar geometrical curvature. The rest, contained within the looped dimension, becomes the electromagnetic force, which does not appear geometrical.

BEYOND EINSTEIN

STRING THEORY

MATTER

MOLECULE

Atoms

ATOM

Nucleus

Neutron

Proton

Electron

Molecules

NEUTRON

Quarks

Strings

Scientists know that everyday matter (like ice) is made of molecules (such as water), and that molecules are made of atoms (including oxygen). Atoms are made of protons, neutrons, and electrons, while protons and neutrons are made up of smaller particles called quarks. Traditionally, quarks and electrons are regarded as point-particles, with zero spatial size. String theorists believe that these "points" are simply the intersection of higher-dimensional loops of energy within the macroscopic plane familiar with humans, similar to how a rubber band intersects almost any two-dimensional plane in a finite number of discrete points.

65

STRING THEORY

The Kaluza–Klein hypothesis of extra dimensions hidden by their compact shape and small size survives today in string theory. What looks like a point-particle in the macroscopic dimensions is actually a one-dimensional string or loop within a microscopic dimension. These strings move and vibrate within space-time. However, because this vibration is within the microscopic dimension that humans cannot directly observe, it does not look like vibration in the usual sense. Instead, physicists observe the motion in the form of characteristics such as mass and charge. String theory describes how vibration affects the interaction among strings, which humans interpret as the laws of physics.[3]

Antigravity

The force of electromagnetism can be attractive or repulsive. Static electricity allows a rubber balloon to pick up paper scraps. It also repels strands of a person's hair away from each other, causing it to stand on end. Yet gravity seems to be only attractive. Why is this? Is there such a thing as repulsive "antigravity?" Electromagnetism has two complementary charges: positive and negative. Like charges repel each other, while opposites attract. Scientists have investigated whether or not there is negative

BEYOND EINSTEIN

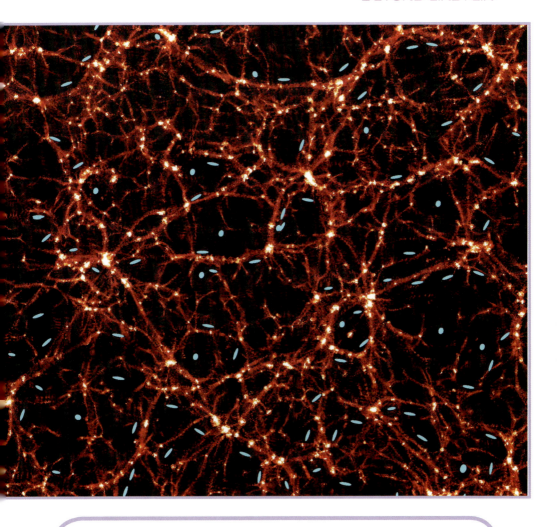

A team from the Paris Astrophysics Institute created a map of dark matter in the universe. The blue shapes are distant galaxies connected by invisible filaments of dark matter, shown in red.

mass so that like masses attract one another through gravity, but opposite masses repel. There are many examples of exotic matter, including antimatter (which "annihilates" standard matter, converting the matter and antimatter into radiation) and dark

GRAVITY EXPLAINED

matter (which is totally invisible, despite being about 86 percent of the matter in the universe). However, none of this exotic matter—or anything theoretically else—has negative mass. Matter always gravitationally attracts matter.

Yet for some reason gravity is causing the familiar stuff of the universe—stars, planets, and so forth—to move away from itself,

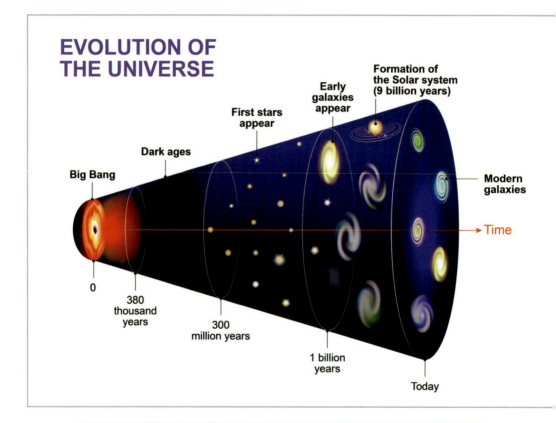

The ultimate fate of the universe depends on gravity. Ever since the big bang, space-time has been being stretched at large scales, causing cosmic expansion. The gravitational attraction of ordinary matter would counteract this growth, causing deceleration or contraction. Instead, the universe continues to grow, and it appears be accelerating.

at least on very large scales. Physicists do not understand the reason, but they have named it dark energy. Dark energy causes space to expand. As space expands, the distance between different galactic clusters grows. The geometry of space-time—gravity—pushes them apart. (Individual galaxies within one cluster are close enough that their attractive gravity overcomes space's expansion.) Surprisingly, as the empty space between clusters grows, the amount of dark energy in the universe increases. The expansion of space becomes faster, while the attraction among clusters grows weaker. Dark energy not only causes the universe to expand and pushes galactic clusters apart, it does so in an accelerating fashion.[4]

Scientists do not know what dark energy is. Some believe it is a mathematical feature (a cosmological constant) in Einstein's equation describing gravity rather than a "thing" present in the universe. Others believe it is a new form of a "thing" unlike anything currently studied in physics. To distinguish this new hypothetical thing from the usual stuff that interacts with the four familiar forces (gravity, electromagnetism, and two nuclear forces), cosmologists, with a show of ironic humor, have given it the name quintessence—the same name Aristotelians gave to the mysterious element they thought kept the stars moving through the sky. Determining what quintessence might be is one of the great adventures of modern physics, inspiring as much excitement today as the mystery of the heavenly bodies did thousands of years ago.

CHAPTER NOTES

Chapter 1.
Early Ideas About Gravity

1. *Oxford Classical Dictionary*, 3rd ed. (2005), s.v. "Aristotle."
2. *Oxford Classical Dictionary*, 3rd ed. (2005), s.v. "element."
3. *Oxford Classical Dictionary*, 3rd ed. (2005), s.v. "Ptolemy (iv)."
4. *Oxford Classical Dictionary*, 3rd ed. (2005), s.v. "astronomy."
5. John Gribbin, *The Scientists: A History of Science Told through the Lives of Its Greatest Inventors* (New York, NY: Random House, 2002), pp. 4–15.
6. Ibid., pp. 50–67.
7. Ibid., pp. 72–103.

Chapter 2.
Isaac Newton and the Law of Universal Gravitation

1. John Gribbin, *The Scientists: A History of Science Told through the Lives of Its Greatest Inventors* (New York: Random House, 2002), pp. 174–180.
2. Ibid., pp. 181–188.
3. John R. Taylor, *Classical Mechanics* (Sausalito, CA: University Science Books, 2005), p. 788.
4. Ibid.
5. Gribbin, pp. 273–275.

CHAPTER NOTES

Chapter 3.
Albert Einstein and the Special Theory of Relativity

1. Edwin F. Taylor and John Archibald Wheeler, *Space-time Physics* (New York, NY: W. H. Freeman and Company, 1992), pp. 84–86.
2. John R. Taylor, *Classical Mechanics* (Sausalito, CA: University Science Books, 2005), p. 788.
3. Silvio Bergia, "Einstein and the Birth of Special Relativity," in *Einstein: A Centenary Volume*, ed. A. P. French (Cambridge, MA: Harvard University Press, 1979), pp. 82–86.
4. J. C. Hafele and R. E. Keating, "Around-the-World Atomic Clocks: Predicted Relativistic Time Gains," *Science* 177, no. 4044 (July 14 1972): pp. 166–168.
5. Bruno Rossi and David B. Hall, "Variation of the Rate of Decay of Mesotrons with Momentum," *Physical Review* 59, no. 3 (February 1941), p. 223.
6. "The Physics of RHIC," Relativistic Heavy Ion Collider, Brookhaven National Laboratory, accessed January 9, 2018, https://www.bnl.gov/rhic/physics.asp.

Chapter 4.
Albert Einstein and the General Theory of Relativity

1. I. Bernard Cohen, "Einstein and Newton," in *Einstein: A Centenary Volume*, A. P. French, ed. (Cambridge, MA: Harvard University Press, 1979), p. 42.

71

GRAVITY EXPLAINED

2. Bernard Schutz, *A First Course in General Relativity* (Cambridge, UK: Cambridge University Press, 2009), p. 113.

Chapter 5.
Experimental Tests of Relativistic Gravity

1. Richard P. Baum and William Sheehan, *In Search of Planet Vulcan: The Ghost in Newton's Clockwork Machine* (New York, NY: Plenum Press, 1997), pp. 127–144.
2. Robert Pound and Glen A. Rebka Jr., "Gravitational Red-Shift in Nuclear Resonance," *Physical Review Letters* 3, no. 9 (November 1, 1959), pp. 439–441.
3. Jay B. Holberg, "Sirius B and the Measurement of the Gravitational Redshift," *Journal for the History of Astronomy* 41, no. 1 (2010), pp. 41–64.
4. Bernard Schutz, *A First Course in General Relativity* (Cambridge, UK: Cambridge University Press, 2009), pp. 227–234.
5. B. P. Abbot, R. Abbott, T. D. Abbott, et al., "Observation of Gravitational Waves from a Binary Black Hole Merger," *Physical Review Letters* 116 (2016), p. 061102.
6. "Lights All Askew in the Heavens," *New York Times*, November 10, 1919, http://graphics8.nytimes.com/packages/pdf/arts/LightsAllAskew.pdf.

Chapter 6.
Beyond Einstein

1. John R. Taylor, *Classical Mechanics* (Sausalito, CA: University Science Books, 2005), pp. 327–330.
2. Ibid., pp. 344–348.
3. Michael E. Peskin and Daniel V. Schroeder, *An Introduction to Quantum Field Theory* (Boulder, CO: Westview Press, 1995), pp. 798–800.
4. Steven Weinberg, *Cosmology* (Oxford, UK: Oxford University Press, 2008), pp. 89–98.

GLOSSARY

acceleration A change in velocity; i.e., a change in speed and/or direction.

curvature A geometrical condition in which initially parallel straight lines fail to remain parallel; the absence of flatness.

curved space-time A space-time in which inertial trajectories (geodesics) that are initially parallel do not necessarily remain parallel.

dark energy A mysterious force causing the universe to expand in an accelerating manner.

Einstein's equation A mathematical law that relates the matter and energy in a space-time with the curvature of the space-time.

Euclidean geometry The kind of geometry used to describe properties of objects in a flat two-dimensional plane; also called plane geometry.

flatness A geometrical condition in which initially parallel straight lines remain parallel; the absence of curvature.

flat space-time A space-time in which initially inertial trajectories (geodesics) that are initially parallel remain parallel.

general relativity Einstein's theory in which matter causes space-time to curve and the curvature of space-time affects how matter moves.

geodesic A curve that does not bend with respect to itself; the shortest distance between two points.

gravitational lensing The bending or magnification of light by a gravitational field.

gravitational wave A ripple in space-time curvature that spreads freely through the universe.

GLOSSARY

inertial motion The motion of a body that is not acted upon by an external force.

inertial observer An observer moving in inertial motion.

length contraction The change in spatial separation between two events in space-time as seen by different observers.

mass The amount of "stuff" making up a physical object. Not to be confused with weight, which is gravitational force acting on mass.

Schwarzschild solution A solution to Einstein's equation that corresponds to the attractive gravitational field around a star or planet.

space-time The mathematical environment, characterized by differences in both spatial distance and time, in which events happen.

special relativity Einstein's theory of motion within flat space-time. It is a special case of general relativity in which space-time is always and everywhere flat.

time dilation The change in time difference between two events in space-time as seen by different observers.

velocity Speed and direction.

weight The gravitational force acting on matter. Not to be confused with mass, which is the amount of "stuff" that the force is acting on.

FURTHER READING

Books

Clark, Stuart. *The Unknown Universe: What We Don't Know About Time and Space.* London, UK: Head of Zeus, 2015.

Czarnecki, Kevin. *Gravity.* New York, NY: Cavendish Square, 2016.

Gilliland, Ben. *Rocket Science for the Rest of Us.* London, UK: Dorling Kindersley, 2015.

Hilton, Lisa. *Gravity, Orbiting Objects, and Planetary Motion.* New York, NY: Cavendish Square, 2017.

Holl, Kristi. *Discovering the Nature of Gravity.* New York, NY: Rosen Young Adult, 2015.

Mussar, George. *Spooky Action at a Distance.* New York, NY: Farrar, Straus and Giroux, 2015.

Wood, Matthew. *The Science of Science Fiction*. White River Junction, VT: Nomad Press, 2017.

FURTHER READING

Websites

Laser Interferometer Gravitational-Wave Observatory (LIGO) Scientific Collaboration
www.ligo.org
Follow the LIGO collaboration as they use gravitational waves to probe the mysteries of the universe, such as colliding neutron stars and black holes.

National Aeronautics and Space Administration (NASA)
www.nasa.gov
Read about the experiments and adventures of America's space program and how astronauts work in weightless conditions orbiting Earth.

Relativity Visualized: Space-time Travel
www.space-timetravel.org
Explore visual computer simulations of relativistic effects such as time dilation and length contraction.

INDEX

A

acceleration, 21–23, 26–27, 29, 43
aether, 33–35
antigravity, 66–69
Aristotle, 10–12, 21
artificial gravity, 61–63
astronauts, 61–63
astronomers, 12–19, 51, 52–54, 56, 59–60

B

black holes, 49–50

C

Cavendish, Henry, 30–31
Copernicus, Nicholas, 14–17
curvature, 6–8, 43–51, 56, 64

D

dark energy, 69
dimensions, extra, 64–66

E

Earth
  motion of, 14–17, 19, 29, 33–35, 53
weight of, 29–31
eclipses, 60
Einstein, Albert
  general relativity and, 8, 42–51, 60
  special relativity and, 32–41, 49
Einstein's equation, 49, 54, 69
epicycles, 12–17
equivalence principle, 27, 43, 61–63
Euclidean geometry, 43–45
experimental testing, 30–31, 33–35, 38–40, 52–60

G

Galileo, 17–19
general relativity, 8, 42–51, 60, 64
geocentricism, 10–14, 19
geodesics, 43–49, 59
Global Positioning System (GPS), 48
gravitational lensing, 59–60
gravitational waves, 7, 49–50, 56–58
gravity
  artificially created, 61–63
  attractive vs. repulsive, 66–69
  early ideas about, 9–19

INDEX

Einstein's theories of, 8, 32–41, 42–51, 60

experimental tests of, 30–31, 33–35, 38–40, 52–60

Newton's laws of, 7, 20–31

H

heliocentrism, 14–19

I

inertial motion, 21, 41, 45–46

inertial observers, 45, 63

inverse-square law, 27–29

K

Kaluza-Klein theory, 64–66

Kepler, Johannes, 16–17

L

Laser Interferometer Gravitational-Wave Observatory (LIGO), 57–58

length contraction, 38–40, 47

light waves, 33–35, 54–56

M

mass, 17, 21–23, 25–31, 42–43, 59–60, 66–68

matter, 6, 8, 17, 21, 43, 48–51, 67–68

Michelson-Morley experiment, 33–35, 56

moons

eclipses and, 60

motion of, 9–12, 19, 26–29

motion

Einstein's theories of, 32–41

inertial motion, 21, 41, 45–46

Newton's laws of, 20–31, 41

of sun, moon, and planets, 9–19, 26–29, 33–35, 52–54

N

Newton, Isaac, 7, 20–31, 41, 42, 48–49, 52–54

O

orbits, 9–19, 26–29, 33–35, 53

P

perihelion shift, 52–54

planets, motion of, 9–19, 28–29, 33–35, 52–54

Ptolemy, 12–14

Q

quantum gravity, 64

R

radioactivity, 39

redshifting, 54–56

79

relativity
  general, 8, 42–51, 60, 64
  special, 32–41, 45, 49

S

Schwarzschild solution, 49
space-time, 35–38, 40–41, 43, 45–50, 52, 56, 64–66
special relativity, 32–41, 45, 49
string theory, 65–66
sun
  eclipses of, 60
  orbits around, 9–19, 33–35, 52–54

T

theories
  general relativity, 8, 42–51, 60, 64
  Kaluza-Klein theory, 64–66
  laws of motion, 20–31, 41
  special relativity, 32–41, 45, 49
  string theory, 65–66
time and space, 35–38, 40–41, 43, 45–50, 52, 56, 64–66
time dilation, 36–38, 40, 47

U

universal gravitation, 7, 20–31

V

velocity, 21–24, 38, 41

W

waves
  gravitational, 7, 49–50, 56–58
  light, 33–35, 54–56
weight, 17–18, 29–31
weightlessness, 61–63